WHAT KATY DID

JOHN BRANSTON

For Rebecca,
who "patched our roof"
and brought sunlight
into our house.
Thanks / Love,

John

First Edition: 2017

All rights reserved.
Copyright © 2017 John Branston

Printed in the United States of America
ISBN 978-0-615-99788-9

for her friends

WHAT KATY DID

Introduction:
Katy and the Mountain Lion

Three years ago my daughter Katy faced down a mountain lion.

She was hiking alone in the mountains of remote western Montana, near where she lived, while her companion went fishing. A careful and experienced hiker, she took her bear spray in her backpack, looked for signs of wildlife, and sang or hollered as she walked. At the top of a ridge she saw a mountain lion on a rock 25 yards away.

She described it in an account she wrote and withheld from me and her mother for weeks until we were safely homeward bound after a visit, knowing we just might take her with us.

"I froze. The cat stood up as soon as it saw me and took a step forward. My immediate instinct was to turn and run, which I did. I had only gone a few steps when I looked back and saw it chasing after me and gaining quickly. The thought flashed through my mind: if I don't stop and face this thing it is going to attack me. I had to show it that I wasn't scared, even though every part of me was telling me otherwise.

"So I did what I never thought I would have the courage or instinct to do. I turned around, grabbed my bear spray, faced the lion with my arms spread wide and let out a giant roar. The lion stopped in its tracks just ten yards from me. Then we had a stare-down for what seemed like ten minutes but was probably more like 10-15 seconds. Neither of us moved as I looked into its dark eyes, hoping to intimidate it. The lion flinched, which reminded me I needed to do something or risk it making the first move. I again spread my arms as wide as I could and roared at the top of my lungs to seem as big and scary as possible. It worked. The lion turned and ran away, disappearing behind the rocks."

Surging with adrenalin but still keeping her head, she sprinted, tumbled, and rock-hopped back to her cabin.

Katy truly had the heart of a lion. But this November, at the age of 29, she lost her life to a different kind of lion – the terrible lion of depression. Knowing for many years that it was inside her, she fought it on her own terms, shunning pills and psychotherapy.

She fought it with goodness. She took jobs working with abused and tormented children, staying with them at night and wrestling them to the ground when necessary as their guardian at school. She energized an after-school program in ways no one had done before. She took a job with Habitat for Humanity of Flathead Valley in Kalispell, Montana. It had been drawing a handful of visitors a week to volunteer at build sites. She bumped it to 30 a week from near and far, then wrote personal notes of thanks to every one of them.

The lion didn't go away. She fought it with lionesque feats of endurance. She biked across the country, leading 32 riders in the Bike and Build nonprofit organization safely from Maine to California. She biked in snow and ice at the seasonal openings and closings of Yellowstone and Glacier National Parks, taunting the lion with friends, laughter, and funny costumes. She raced down ski slopes, plunged into icy lakes, dipped in remote hot springs. She taught herself to play guitar and ukulele. She danced. She loved. She cried. She tried. Oh how she tried.

But this lion is crafty. It waits and watches. It leaves you alone, for weeks, maybe months, then sneaks up on you in the middle of the night, sits on your chest, and whispers in your ear, "you're a failure, you're not enough, you let people down."

The lion is especially active around Thanksgiving and Christmas, when the days are short, the nights long, and everyone is happy and gay except for those who are distraught and can't bear the thought of going through the motions one more time.

So now the lion is in our home, our hearts, and our heads. And will be for a long, long time. I hope to live as bravely as Katy did. If you don't stop and face this thing it is going to attack you.

* * *

"Life is amazing. And then it's awful. And then it's amazing again. And in between the amazing and the awful it's mundane and ordinary and routine. Breathe in the amazing, hold on through the awful, and relax and exhale during the ordinary. That's just living heart-breaking, soul-healing amazing, awful, ordinary life. And it's breathtakingly beautiful."
—author L.R. Knost, from the first page of Katy's notebook

"We have all hurt someone tremendously, whether by intent or accident, we have all loved someone tremendously, whether by intent or accident. It is an intrinsic human trait, and a deep responsibility, I think, to be an organ and a blade. But, learning to forgive ourselves and others because we have not chosen wisely is what makes us most human. We make horrible mistakes. It's how we learn. We breathe love. It's how we learn. And it is inevitable."
—Nayyirah Waheed, in Katy's journal entry in 2016

"It was hard to grasp that a person I leaned upon for comfort and support was hurting in such a deep way."
—Kristen Ewing, New York, Katy's friend
and fellow cross-country bike tripper

"Immediately ask the question the story is going to answer: what are you doing and why?"

—Katy's journal for her writing class, 2015

* * *

How Could She?

How could someone who could coax other people to get up at five in the morning, motivate them to go to school or bike 100 miles before sunset, ignore thunderstorms and exhaustion, and put a smile on their faces while doing it take her own life?

How could someone so brave and joyous and loved and seemingly upbeat be so sad and depressed? Or maybe the question is not "how could she be" but "how could she not be" because somehow they go together.

This is clearer to me now as I remember her letters, journals, blogs, and emails that are too painful to explore, too important to ignore.

Katy was an organizer. She organized meals and activities for parties and visitors, "Katy bucket-list" itineraries for trips, daily duties for a 75-day Bike and Build ride across America, jobs for Habitat volunteers, and her own life for a book. She was an inspiration and comfort to so many others. She was a leader who could move other people to push beyond their expectations and achieve higher goals. But she struggled under the burden of the lion with the big life decisions of choosing a college, career, a life partner, and a place to live.

In early 2016, when things were not going well, she began keeping a journal and writing an outline and timetable for "a book that I am going to write by June 1, 2017 (my 30th birthday) that will consist of stories and lessons I have learned in the first 30 years of my life. Because I am at a crossroads in my life where I find myself inspired to write and to create. I will do it by writing my ass off, wherever and whenever to *make it happen*."

June 1ˢᵗ, 2017: "SHARE THE BOOK!"

She grouped her extended family and her friends from her Memphis childhood, high school, college at Elon in North Carolina, Missoula, Whitefish, Bike and Build, and her jobs. She would include everyone she had loved, in her words and theirs. She set a timetable for finishing it by June of 2017. There are names and reference I don't recognize and others that are none of my business. Her notes make it clear though that she intended to write about her demons as well as her good times.

Katy outlined the book when she was living in Whitefish, Montana, working for Habitat for Humanity of Flathead Valley, and battling depression. She did not finish it. She took her life in November of 2016 when she was 29 years old. The false start at the book was perhaps a form of therapy. I don't know because she did not tell me about it. I found her notes after she died.

So it has fallen to me to finish it for her.

For her, and for me, and for her many friends who knew her happy, energetic side but probably not her dark side.

I am an unreliable narrator. I want to emphasize that this book, excepting the italicized material at the beginning of each chapter, is my view as Katy's father. This is especially true of the part about Katy's childhood and upbringing. Writing is my therapy.

I did not understand her dark side very well myself, but I knew it was there and she was fighting it with the heart of a lion. Somewhere I read that serious depression is not something that comes over you, it lives inside you constantly, a chemical imbalance. If I did not really understand this then how can I expect her friends to? When I read the hundreds of sensitive, thoughtful letters and cards of condolence after her death, I cry over them, then reread them and cry some more. Two months after her death, the mailman still delivers a boxful of tears every day. But most of them are one-dimensional, like an album that only includes pictures of celebrations.

Katy was more complicated, self-aware, and troubled. Most of her friends in Montana and places far away – 1007 of them on Facebook – thought she was living the dream, hiking and biking in Glacier and Yellowstone national parks in the summer and fall and skiing in the winter. No wonder. Few if any of them knew or suspected how much she was hurting. Barely two months before she died she posted eight sunny "bikepacking" photos and the line "Really...how many times can I feel like I'm in Heaven during my lifetime?" She always shared her happiness. She almost never shared her depression. She fought the lion alone, on her own terms.

In her room and office she posted a card that said "A person who feels appreciated will always do more than what is expected." and another that said "Your smile is your logo, your personality is your business card, how you leave others feeling after having an experience with you becomes your trademark."

Why did I not understand this better? Maybe it's because fathers do not know their sons and daughters, and vice versa, or know them in different ways than friends. Or maybe it was blindness or thoughtlessness on my part. Or both. How different the two of us were – Katy spontaneous, bold, a joyful dancer; me calculating, cautious, cranky, irritable, a bookish would-be writer. When I sensed her struggle, I wrote "Dad Letters" of wise and witty advice that were about as helpful to her as an aspirin or a get-well card from Hallmark.

I should have pressed harder against her denial and mine. I should have helped her in so many ways. But would it have saved her? I can't say.

Katy was unsure what she wanted to be in a career sense but knew exactly what she wanted to be like: her mother, as loving and selfless a person as I have ever known. Jenny spent five days with her a week before she took her life, and Katy seemed to be pulling herself out of her blackness. She wrote an upbeat note to her and stuffed it in her suitcase where Jenny found it after she got home. We were confident that she would come home for Thanksgiving on the plane ticket she had already purchased.

When she died she was alone in a rented house shared with three people she did not know well. Kind people, good people, but not close friends. Her best friends were hundreds or thousands of miles away, and her closest Montana friends were unaware of the urgency of her depression and how hard she was fighting the lion that was closing in on her. Her brother Jack was in his third year of medical school in Hawaii. Jenny and I had just bought a second home on the Mississippi Gulf Coast, unknowingly snuffing out Katy's faint hope that we would move nearer to her in Montana. She had tested the online dating site Match.com., which was totally against her nature and must have made her feel even worse about herself. She was moving for the third time in less than a year. She was under deadline pressure to get volunteers to complete two houses by mid December (which they did, we learned later). She had just been forced out of her apartment after her six-month lease ran out and her landlord refused to extend it to the end of the year. The week she moved out her purse was stolen.

She was closing in on 30 and unmarried although she had attended a half dozen weddings within the last two years. Winter was coming. She was unhappy and overworked in her job. She didn't know what she wanted to be, much less how to get there. Her breakup with the man she loved was final after a reconciliation didn't take.

"I just want a nice place to live and someone to share it with," she told me in our last phone call.

Mom went to the rescue. Katy began taking anti-depressants

and set appointments with a therapist and a doctor she had seen previously. But it wasn't enough. We kick ourselves now for not insisting that she come home to Memphis, for not staying with her longer, for not physically forcing her to get professional treatment. And we wonder if any of that would have made any difference.

I knew how badly she was hurting and as her father I could not stop her. I say that simply as a statement of fact, although there were several instances when, in hindsight, I could have acted and spoken and written more forcefully than I did. Since her death I have been told and read many times that suicide survivors should not blame themselves. But I can't believe it, not yet, maybe not ever. I read Dr. Karl Menninger's observation in *Man Against Himself* by way of Joan Didion's *Blue Nights* (I could not concentrate on longer books) about "the apparent inadequacy of the precipitating event" when trying to understand a suicide. I got stuck on that. But not in the way it was intended. There seemed to me no shortage of adequate precipitating events, and if only...

If only. Suicide is such a guilt-fest.

Two months after her death I am still afraid to face the lion. I read the sympathy cards, cry with friends, trade e-mails, look at the Facebook tributes, place pictures of her smiling face in every room and on my computer. Hardest for me are the things that evoke her everyday life – the one-word e-mail responses to me on her computer that say "fine" or "ok". Her prescriptions and her journals and her pocketbook with the receipt for the pizzas she bought for friends the weekend before she died. The bike helmet and jersey in a box upstairs that still carry her scent and strands of her hair. The handwritten birthday cards I keep in the drawer next to the bed. The articles I read and instinctively want to email to her, like the one about how to take a "volunteering vacation" so she could read them at work and smile and write back, "Thanks, Dad., already saw it."

This is a short book that can be read in a hour or two, which is fine because that's about all I have in the tank and Katy wouldn't want us moping around. Katy believed in living true. I wrote this for her as well as for myself and her family and friends and, perhaps, others who are battling their own demons and did not have the privilege of knowing her.

1: Growing Up in the House of Games

"I was blessed to know Katy most of my life and she was one of the strongest people I ever knew. Katy was one of the few people I knew when I came to White Station High School as a freshman. She went out of her way to make me feel welcome and helped me make friends. With all my heart I wish I could have helped her when she needed it most."

—Phillip Brooks, Nashville

" Katy introduced me to the band Nickle Creek on our daily morning carpool to high school before I had a driver's license. I fell in love with one of the songs so much that I have planned to use it as part of my upcoming wedding reception. Nickle Creek is part of the sound track of my high school experience, all because of Katy. She was one of the most genuinely kind people I have ever known. Even as a teenager when everyone was trying to be cool and prove themselves to each other Katy was simply herself. And everyone loved her for it. She had a way of making everyone around her feel comfortable, loved, and accepted."

—Shelly Ramsey, Memphis

* * *

Katy.

That's the name my wife and I chose for our second child in

1987. We chose it because it had a simple, straightforward, energetic honesty to it that seemed promising. There was no family connection, but it went well with Jack, the name of her older brother born in 1984. She was Katherine on the paperwork, but nobody called her that. She was just Katy or KK to her friends and Katy Boo, Boopster or Boo to me and Jenny. That was plenty.

My friend Rheta Grimsley Johnson likes to say that "some people have all the luck" when she hears about an author or songwriter who had a childhood of hardship and suffering. It's a funny line with some truth to it. Pain and adversity can toughen you and make your story interesting to other people, just as an ideal family can be a bore as well as a burden because, of course, there is no such thing. Childhood memories, even the happiest ones, are not trustworthy. Details fade into confusion. Moods are tricky. Were you happy on that family road trip, or bored with the scenery, the company, the music, and secretly wishing you were some place else? Were you at peace on that walk in the woods or just lonely? Were you in love with those old friends or secretly jealous, insecure, and out of place? Time and nostalgia put a gloss over things.

But our family had so much luck. If we didn't win the life lottery we came awfully close. A good house at a good price on a good street in a good neighborhood with a good public school in a gritty city that gave you a fighting chance and favored families like ours. Katy was a grateful beneficiary. A neighborhood Gang of Three – KatyKateandRachel – bonded as one name from the age of three, friends for life. Good health. Katy the naughty tot who once hid her dinner peas in her mouth for half an hour while riding in the car, Jack the big brother who suspected something was up and tricked her into opening her mouth and spitting out the damning evidence. Parents who stayed together and loved being parents. Homemade Halloween costumes and a mural painted on the bedroom wall. Dachshunds Coco and her successor Abby that got in bed with her. A pink baby-blanket-for-life named "Bubby." Bedtime stories by Audrey Wood and Chris Van Allsburg, *Heckety Peg* and *The Polar Express*, *The Wizard of Oz* and "Darfy" on the VCR, singalong with Raffi, butterfly kisses, g'nite bite, sleep tight, and see you in the morning, in the morning, ever and ever in the morning.

Yearly road trips in unreliable station wagons and minivans to Seagrove Beach, Florida before 30A became a bumper sticker and to Michigan with lakes and sand dunes like nothing in the South.

A "Papaw" in south Mississippi with hard edges and a thick accent Katy learned to imitate when he called on the phone. *Dixie Gardens* with its Rainbow Barn that was an Interstate 55 landmark before it fell down, a swimming pool with a diving board for follow the leader, a tennis court gouged out of red clay with a bulldozer and groomed with a Buick in its infancy, a pond that reflected the sunsets, and a three-person swing hanging from a pecan tree.

The stories and tall tales about Sonny the high-diver or Shag the football hero or Jigger and the Germans in WWII or Ernest at Parchman Penitentiary or Minnie across the road and her chickens fighting off Papaw's bird dogs. Stories to be told over and over at dinner, which meant lunch, which was made by Rosie the cook who lived with her husband Willie in a trailer with no air conditioner. The world of poor whites and poorer blacks, tractors, old trucks stained with mud and cow shit and chewing tobacco, critters that got under the house and made a stink, monstrous snakes that might or might not have been seen by farm hand Eddie Junior or his father and even bigger liar Big Eddie, droughts to gripe about, rising creeks to worry about, mama cows to look after, bulls to watch out for, hay bales to climb on, timber to be harvested, saw mills and stockyards, longleaf pines, hardwood bottoms, and of course guns and hunting.

We raised Katy and Jack retro and proud, and a lot of it stuck. Ours was a house of games.

Fortunately, Katy was born before electronic devices ruled the world. We did our best to inoculate her against them, but we were such innocents. The first computer game we owned was called Crystal Quest, and one night we came home and discovered that the babysitter had the top 20 scores, so we stopped using her. We were late to computers, video games, Nintendo, Super Mario, Pac Man, Donkey Kong, gamers, DVDs, Facebook, Myspace, high def, LED, wall-mounted, big-screen, and 2.0. We held on to playing cards, board games, balls, books, typewriters, and word processors.

Katy was unbeatable at games after she learned the rules. After she outgrew Candy Land and Chutes and Ladders and moved up to the big leagues, we made them increasingly complicated, even borderline insane, but she figured them out anyway. She killed at hearts, spades, crazy eights, four-card, ninety-nine, spelling bees, Monopoly, Scrabble, Sudoku, and cribbage. She never owned a television after college, and liked to write letters on a vintage typewriter she found at a thrift store. Better than games were pranks, skits, stunts, costume parties, $5 prom dresses, any sport in which you could goof off and wear a costume, karaoke, and ping pong.

School was a snap for her. She never made a B, but there were the normal highs and lows. Our first big parental school decision was taking her out of our neighborhood elementary school, Snowden, after fifth grade and putting her in a school farther away that was a gateway to the most desirable (and whitest) middle and high schools. I think Katy had some regrets. She didn't want the pressure or phoniness of being cool. She wore Oshkosh overalls and unfashionable shoes. She had black and white friends. Her favorite teacher begged her and us to stay. I took a morning off from work one day to watch her compete in the Snowden spelling bee as one of the fifth-graders taking on the middle-schoolers. One after one, the contestants were eliminated until it was just her and an eighth-grader up on the stage. The kids in the auditorium were roaring. Damn, I realized, they're cheering for Katy. She is their champion, and I'm taking her away. She's betraying them.

The awkward pre-teen years are when parents are supposed to be parents and point the way. In our house we had another kind of life-defining family experience.

Some time in 1998 I was smitten by one of my annual brainstorms to take a romantic weekend trip minus the kids to an exciting new destination within 250 miles of Memphis. We had lived in Memphis since 1982 so it was not easy to do this. I settled on a bed-and-breakfast inn with a horsey western theme outside of Nashville. The deal included a "trail ride" over the scenic hills of Williamson County, a sack lunch, a quick riding lesson, and an opportunity to bond with our horses. The sack lunch, as I remember, was a bag of chips and a miniature Snickers and the equine bonding translated to washing down the horses, which never broke a sweat, after the ride. But the trip was a life-changing success because we discovered *Seinfeld*. Yes, in the year the most popular comedy of the decade went off the air, we discovered it, just in time for the finale. In the next ten years, we made up for it by watching reruns as a family every night at dinner time until we all knew the plots, lines, and gags by heart. "Oh, Rusty!" when someone farted. "If the homeless don't like 'em, the homeless don't have to eat 'em" when someone didn't clean their plate. "Thanks George, I never had a Big Mac before" if dinner was leftovers. "I got nothin'!" "Serenity Now!" "If this van's a rockin' don't come a knockin.'"

We took *Seinfeld* to heart if not too far. I was Jerry, Jenny or sometimes Katy was Elaine, Jack was George, our dachshund Abby was Kramer, and our despised and mean cat Skittles was Newman. Along with Monty Python, Mr. Bean, and Will Farrell's sketches on *Saturday Night Live*, this was what passed for family entertainment at the Branston household during Katy and Jack's adolescence. A proud legacy, if you have seen Katy do Spartan Cheerleaders or the

Circle of Life birth scene from *The Lion King* or karaoke.

I emphasize that this world view, or partial world view, was mine, not necessarily anyone else's. Jenny has learned to live with me but she is and always was a faithful person, in the best sense of the word. I was aware that there was a moral emptiness at the bottom of life as *Seinfeld*. In the last episode, the characters just walk away in different directions after serving time in jail for "criminal indifference." There was nothing to hold on to in the dark hours, nothing to believe in beyond the healing power of laughter and recognition of absurdity.

Which is actually quite a lot, and the older I get the more I believe it. Katy was a born ham, with a little help from her friends. As I proudly said in a toast on some festive occasion years later, "this is the sort of cruel humor and merciless family abuse that made her the person she is today."

I think she agreed, or at least she laughed when I said it.

2: Interlude with Music

"I was in an a cappella group at Elon and Katy was undoubtedly our biggest fan. She was at every show, screaming and cheering, and she knew all the words. She often "fake auditioned" for me and wondered what it would be like to be a Sweet Signature. Her enthusiasm meant so much to me and the other girls in my group. When we were sophomores, Katy and I lived together. My dad gave me a guitar and I brought it back to Elon, and I began to learn basic chords. Soon I was playing songs. Lots of friends asked me to teach them how to play, and I did, but they lost interest. Not Katy. I could almost see sparks in her eyes when I taught her the first few chords. Before I knew it, she was borrowing my guitar and learning songs on her own. I still remember watching TV in our common room one night and hearing Katy belting out "Chasing Cars" in her room with the door closed. As for the ukulele, one of my boyfriends gave me a ukulele for Christmas about four or five years ago, and I would usually see Katy around the holidays if she was home from Montana. I had a chord book and showed her how to play a few chords. The first song I ever learned was "I'm Yours" by Jason Mraz, and that's the first song she sings on her YouTube video."
—Lizzie Napier, Nashville

"When we moved in together in Missoula in 2012, I had a ukulele that I had brought from Hawaii. Katy wasn't paying much guitar at the time but got really interested in the ukulele because she liked the sound and because the chords

were easier for smaller hands than on a guitar. She was totally self taught and would play for me often as she chose songs to cover. She got to the point where she probably had 20 or so songs down pretty much perfectly. She began to play for others as time progressed and she became more comfortable. Once she picked up the ukulele, I rarely ever saw her play the guitar again. She loved the ukulele."

—Dylan, Whitefish

"Katy's motive for learning the uke was basic and so true to her nature. She wanted something portable, that she could take on bikepacking, backpacking, or river trips. Both the uke and the guitar are ideal complements to outdoor environs, unobtrusive enough to feature simply as background noise, but also with the power to draw people in around the campfire or add to the pleasure of floating a calm stretch of water. Ukes also tended to show up at Ultimate Frisbee tournaments. In fact, during one of the first tournaments we attended together, a gorgeous young man on an opposing team charmed all the ladies with his post-game ukulele serenades. He kept turning up at tournaments and became a legend known simply as "Ukulele Guy." We all had massive crushes on him."

—Angela Mallon, Missoula

"Listen to the music of the moment people, dance and sing
We're just one big family
And it's our God-forsaken right to be loved loved love love"
Lyrics from "I'm Yours" by Jason Mraz

* * *

We were not a musical family in the sense of being able to actually play instruments. Jenny took piano lessons as a girl and can play pretty well when she puts her mind to it. I wish I could write songs and sing like Stevie Wonder. Jack is a really good fisherman.

Katy took band as an elective in middle school. The alternative must have been something like bug collecting because she had previously indicated no talent or interest in this direction. Her instrument of choice was the flute because that's what her friend Rachel played. But the strategy backfired when they got put in different lunch hours, and the flute investment did not take despite the efforts of an excellent band teacher. At Christmas break Katy was supposed to take her flute home and practice every day. The flute never left its black box.

On the night of the my-kid-is-so-special concert we beamed with pride as Katy tooted away in the back row on John Phillip Sousa or the *Theme from Star Wars* under cover of the percussion and horn sections. Years later she 'fessed up. In the best tradition of Milli Vanilli and the boy bands, she had faked it.

I put the flute on craigslist but it didn't sell. I still have it. No reasonable offer will be refused.

Her college friend Lizzie planted the seed that bloomed in Montana when Katy took up the ukulele. I only know two things about the instrument – a strange dude named Tiny Tim played one on the *Tonight Show* back in the Johnny Carson years and it was often misspelled by newspaper reporters and corrected by copy editors.

Katy practiced and got better, playing mostly for her own enjoyment or for close friends. Jack captured her on his camera at Thanksgiving 2015 singing and playing "Walking in Memphis" and "I'm Yours" by Jason Mraz and sent it to us as a holiday surprise. She played with passion, by herself, expressing emotion she could not put in words. In summer, she accompanied herself at the Habitat for Humanity build site playing her song "Build Day" to the tune of "My Girl" for the amusement of the volunteers.

She also started collecting vintage record albums, shopped for a turntable, and played Motown on Pandora over and over. I believe this was a loving nod to her retro-loving Pops from Michigan.

The uke now belongs to her special five-year-old mini-me buddy Lucy Downing in Whitefish. Katy was teaching her to play, and her picture is on the back.

3: High Grades and High Anxiety

"I met Katy in 2006 when I learned that she had applied for Lakeshore staff and also went to Elon where I would be going that fall. We were both on staff at Lakeshore in 2007 and 2008 and at Elon she was my mentor in the Honors Program. She was the only person I knew as a freshman, and she made me feel so welcomed, so much like I belonged. She did the same for campers at Lakeshore. Kids always felt accepted around her. Come to think of it, I think everyone who knew her felt welcomed and known by her. I wanted to tell you how much Katy meant to me. Regretfully, I am not sure that I ever communicated that to her. Katy was such a light in my life over the last decade, in some times when I really needed it. She impacted so many more lives than you will probably ever hear about. But know that her influence was strong, and I am one of the many who will strive to continue to carry her light in this world, to live out the things that she taught us."

—Katie Strickland Swift, Seattle

"Katy was my first friend at Elon. We lived across the hall from each other in the Staley dormitory. She fondly started calling me "Dodo" after I messed up an icebreaker we were playing with some Staley girls on the first day of school. That night she barged into my room in a panic after trying out some new face wash. She was holding her bright red face and shouting "my face! It's stinging!" And that's how I gave her the nickname 'Stingface'. I will never forget how she

supported me during one of my hardest times at Elon. She was there for me when I felt the most alone. She supported my crazy decision to switch from broadcast communications to nursing. She mailed me my first pair of scrub pants when I started nursing school. What I love most about my friendship with Katy was how we could always pick up right where we left off. Because soulmates are forever."

—Lizzie Napier, Nashville

"I had the privilege of getting to know Katy when she interned with us at the Redwoods Group. Even though she only worked here that summer, it's still easy to remember the positive energy and joy she brought to everyone she worked with and how she made the most of everything she did. The way she gave so much to others was a big part of why, when we realized she would be celebrating her 21st birthday alone after training camp counselors in the middle of Pennsylvania, a few of us did not hesitate to rearrange our travel plans so that we could meet her and take her out to dinner in Philadelphia to celebrate. That is still one of the best moments I've had during my ten plus years here, and one of so many ways that Katy brought people together and brought joy to them."

—Dan Baum, Raleigh

* * *

Making straight A's in school is overrated.

It takes smarts, but in a public high school in Memphis it can also be a sign of easy courses, undemanding teachers, and grade inflation. All of that was part of the mix at White Station High School, a magnet school for college-bound students. Make enough A's over several years and they become a burden – the burden of perfection.

Jenny and I were not hover parents. We let Katy make her own way while supporting her, going to her games, and encouraging her to explore new places and meet people. She had good habits. We never had to get her out of bed or push her to do her homework or worry about who she was hanging out with. She was grateful for the good teachers and coaches, slept through the easy courses, and navigated the crowded hallways and cliques without trouble.

Picking a college was hard. She had no particular interest in science, music, or math that would have made the choice easier or at least narrowed the possibilities. Like me, she wanted to go to a liberal arts college or university, preferably one with around 5000 students. Rhodes College in Memphis was too close and too small. The University of Tennessee-Knoxville was too big. Vanderbilt was too expensive. Its Nashville neighbor, Belmont, which I saw as the budget alternative, was too much of a comedown. Sewanee was too isolated and elitist. UNC-Asheville was affordable but sort of weird. Western Carolina was too ordinary.

So we took a second college tour to eastern North Carolina. We looked at Duke, North Carolina at Chapel Hill, Wake Forest, Davidson, and finally Elon, an hour west of Durham. And the search was over. Love at first sight. An enrollment of 4500. A welcoming speaker who remembered people's names and called them by name. An Honors College that offered her a $12,000 a year scholarship. A semester abroad. A sticker price of $25,000 a year, all included. A pretty campus with lots of green grass, a lake, a small town, a day's drive from Memphis, and not a soul that she knew, which did not bother her a bit.

She made friends in the freshman dormitory, liked her mentor in the Honors College, made straight As, and only came home once, at Christmas break. In sophomore year, however, there were cracks. She lived in an apartment with seven other girls, all of whom joined sororities except for Katy. She found her identity instead in the no-coaches, no-refs sport of Ultimate Frisbee. She organized and captained the club team.

But something was bothering her. The demon was visiting. It

was time to pick a major, to think about a job after college, a future, an adult life.

"I can picture us sitting in the parking lot of the main library the summer after sophomore year of college and just crying our eyes out together," her Memphis friend Lindsay Morris remembers. "She was feeling so hopeless. She didn't know what direction to go in college and felt this unexplainable weight on her. She had had ups and downs with college friends/roommates/boys, but even she could identify that it was bigger than that. Nothing seemed to be enough. That was the first time I can remember really seeing the depth of her sadness, but it is only in retrospect that I realize it was truly deep."

Jenny and I did not see the deep hurt that Katy showed Lindsay. We had each had our own good and bad college experiences and figured that was part of the deal. At a time when we walking on the thin ice of middle age and self-employment, Katy's college career was our rock, our vicarious adventure, something we could think about, talk about, and brag about with pure pride.

In her junior year, Katy did a semester abroad at the University for Foreigners Perugia in Italy. If this sounds familiar, here's why: Amanda Knox and the ultimate more-than-I-bargained-for semester abroad.

Amanda Knox, also 20 years old at the time, was an exchange student in Perugia who was convicted in Italy of stabbing to death her British roommate after a night of sex and drugs. Her conviction was overturned after she spent four years in prison, and she wrote a book about her experience.

There was a total immersion college and another for one-and-done international students who did not speak fluent Italian. Katy did not know Amanda Knox but it was, of course, impossible to not be aware of her because she was an even bigger story in the Italian media than she was back home. The Elon coeds, we later learned, avoided telling their parents much about this for fear of alarming them, but some of them stayed in their apartments until the arrest.

Katy had her own extracurricular adventures. How much, if at all, she and other young women were influenced by the Knox story I do not know. Katy didn't dwell on it in her emails or with Jenny when she came and visited. My guess is that it was roughly equivalent to living in San Francisco during the Summer of Love in 1967 for my generation.

The things Katy wrote to us about were more mundane, and her tone was usually upbeat: her first long bike ride through the Umbria countryside, speaking Italian, eating gelato, gaining 15 pounds, ripping a pair of expensive jeans, dyeing her hair black, living in a cramped apartment, Italian men, seeing the sights, the exhilarating and anxiety-producing strangeness of it all.

In a journal she kept for a writing class years later, she hinted at other adventures while she was in Italy. Maybe she was just heeding the instructor's advice to "write more than warm fuzzies" and "build a story around a search for something." Or maybe not. She was introspective, then as always.

"In that moment," she wrote, "I took a deep breath and realized I was in the Italy of my imagination and I was completely and hopelessly lost."

If she completed that chapter of her book I have not found it. On balance, I think her time in Italy was life-changing. She wasn't on her own, but she was far from the support and comforts of Memphis and Elon. She was doing what she thought she should do – challenging herself and getting out of her comfort zone so she could be the adult she wanted to be.

Back at Elon, she was a tour guide and got to meet anchorman Brian Williams and historian David McCullough. She earned a summer internship with an insurance company that gave her use of a car and sent her on the road to inspect YMCA facilities all over the northeastern United States. A "big girl" job – and a more stressful one than we knew – that would surely be a career-opener.

The Ultimate Team grew in numbers and skill as it attracted athletic students looking for something different. The women's team bonded, and chose the name Free To Lay. They made up cheers for the opposing teams, always ending in "you're pretty." In their last home game, they came from behind to score the winning point on a "huck" from Katy to one of her roommates and won a spot in the regionals. A crowd had gathered as the men's game ended and word of the comeback spread. Jenny was among those watching and was so excited she ran on to the field and turned a cartwheel, becoming a legend in her own right.

At the graduation ceremony in 2009, Katy and Page and Emily posed in the courtyard for pictures in their caps and gowns and mingled with the parents for a couple of hours. It was only our fourth or fifth time on the campus in four years. We didn't know anyone. We were like freshmen. Quite a few instructors and administrators came up to us and introduced themselves to say how much they enjoyed Katy. She should have been on top of the world.

But at a party at her apartment that night she was subdued. I remember her opening letters from family members who sent her cards and generous checks. One, for $800, was from my 92-year-old aunt in Florida, whom Katy had never met. Another was from my stepmother in Michigan on behalf of my late father, another from my sister in California. As Katy read the notes, I noticed she was crying and her hands were shaking. "I don't deserve this," she said softly.

All those honors, all those good grades, all that praise – what a burden. The burden of high expectations. A burden of perfection, of never failing but still failing somehow. She felt that.

I doubt if she ever had a conversation in Italian after college. But the hook was set that semester in Perugia, in more ways than one. There was something to this distance biking business. There was a big world outside the Southeastern United States. She would go out and see it, first in a camper truck, then on a bike.

4: Summer Camp: Lion King and The Big Kahuna

"I first met Katy at Camp Lakeshore when I was eight. I was timid, scared, I never talked, I was hiding secrets from a dysfunctional family that were weighing me down. I was in no mood to make friends. But Katy was relentless, and she won me over. I was scared to hike up Pilot's Knob in the night. I was scared of the dark. Katy held my hand the whole way, she told me stories and she listened to my stories. I think I talked more to Katy than I ever had to anyone. I wanted to be just like her. I wanted to be a counselor like Katy at camp, I wanted to know everything I could about high ropes, I wanted to fearlessly travel. I begged her to teach me things and she always did. After my first week at camp Katy wrote me letters almost weekly. She gave me something to look forward to. I would check the mail daily and when I saw a letter with my name on it I would run to the top of the driveway and sit under the stairs and read of Katy's adventures and the encouraging words she gave me. Sometimes I got letters from Cousin Clementine who I eventually figured out was Katy. I still have those letters and treasure them. Sometimes I read them and think of how much one person impacted where my life was going. One year I applied to be on staff as the Ropes or Nature director. But I was not hired that year. I was going to just stay home, convinced that I would never belong anywhere but Lakeshore, but naturally Katy was there for me again, telling me to listen to those tiny voices in the back of my head that gave me crazy ideas like going to a different camp to work, somewhere I had never been. A month later I found myself boarding a plane for southern New Mexico,

equally excited and terrified, but knowing I wanted some sense of adventure Katy embodied to well. I am just one person in an ocean's worth of people that Katy impacted. I am one person, but there are so many more like me out there, people who can say Katy was someone who deserves credit for getting to where we are now. In another month I will leave Guam and come back to the states. I will go back to the kindergarten and first-graders I have taught at an inner-city after-school program throughout college and I will tell them stories of a hero who lived a life of unimaginable adventure and service to others, who put good into the world every day. I can only hope she knew how much she meant to me."

—Katie Mobley, Guam

"Katy and I worked together for a summer at Camp Seafarer on the coast of North Carolina. She was a joy and a light. We have, each summer, a big competition at camp in the second half of the season when the heat is high and everyone is mentally and physically tired. It's called the Big Kahuna Cup. Katy and her small staff at the Environmental Discovery Center came up with the most creative and enthusiastic programs that made the children excited to learn, and it was hilarious and inspiring. Just like Katy. Needless to say, they won the whole competition and Katy was crowned The Big Kahuna and that is how I will always remember her."

—Meredith Stewart, Durham

* * *

Camp was as much of a respite for Katy as it was for the campers. For two summers when she was in college Katy worked at Camp Lakeshore on the Tennessee River two hours east of Memphis. She was a lifeguard one summer and in charge of the Ropes Program the next. She was Staff Member of the Year the first summer. Her highlights, preserved on YouTube, include a spoof of Will Farrell's klutzy Spartan cheerleaders skit and a rendition of the "Lion King" birth scene "Circle of Life" in which she strikes a heroic pose, thrusts an arm in the air, and belts our a war cry while suppressing a grin. You have to watch them to appreciate. The Ropes Program was designed to help kids overcome their fear of physical challenges and heights. As the camper describes, Katy was good at that.

The summer before her senior year at Elon Katy worked at Camp Seafarer on the coast of North Carolina. It was considered a prize job at a sailing camp for privileged kids, but Katy didn't know anyone or anything about sailing and was assigned to the less exciting environmental center and the youngest campers. She took it as a challenge and rose to the occasion.

5: Moving to Montana

"Today is my six-year Montanaversary. When I moved to Montana six years ago I wanted to live in a vibrant mountain town, make friends and a life for myself. I got a job, a roommate and the beginnings of a new life in Montana. Then I had a breakdown, quit my job and left without telling anyone. I was having suicidal thoughts and even went so far as to walk to the river with the intent to throw myself in and hopefully die of hypothermia or drowning. I didn't go through with it but that event led me to book a plane ticket to Memphis and ditch town shortly after. I don't want this to happen again, but I am scared."

—Katy's journal entry, Dec. 6, 2015

"I woke this morning to the season's first snow in the valley. At midday a fox ran by my office window, its red coat muted by the low angle sunlight. I work just down the street from Hawthorne Elementary, where I once helped Katy coach a Flagship Program running club. Her picture hangs above my desk, the one of her deep blue eyes framed by the frozen lashes and a pair of reflective goggles. That winter we skied together around town, rescuing cars stuck in snow drifts up to our hips during a February blizzard. As we swooshed across the Orange Street Bridge over the Clark Fork River illuminated by street lights, I thought 'that girl is one of my most treasured friends. I will remember this night as long as I live. And I will."

—Angela Mallon, Missoula

"I am so grateful for the example Katy set for my daughter of how to be a woman in the world. She introduced Josie to Ultimate, to costume parties, and 'Mean Girls'. She celebrated Josie, and Jo delighted in her. They had a really special connection. Katy lived with us when Josie was in fourth grade and I think her influence helped Josie move into the middle school years with confidence in herself. Katy made everything more fun, shinier, and more meaningful. She made everyone feel good and she made the world better. She just sparkled."

—Lisa Firehammer, Missoula

* * *

Missoula is the place where 20-somethings go to retire.

I laughed when I read that somewhere, then my own two 20-somethings moved to Missoula.

Nobody in our family had ever even been to Montana. I knew it as the Big Sky place where Phil Jackson played basketball, Custer made his last stand, and Texas Rangers Woodrow Call and Augustus McRae drove a herd of cattle in *Lonesome Dove*.

When Katy graduated summa cum laude from Elon she had a degree in communications and no idea what she wanted to do. So she and her friends Allie and Nikki from the Ultimate Frisbee team decided to take a summer cross-country road trip. One of their family's owned a truck camper they named Lance and away they went. That was Cross Country Katy 1.0.

Lance and Co. visited Missoula. A year earlier Jack had moved there after having enough of being a fishing guide in Alaska for three summers. He strapped a canoe on top his battered SUV, pulled up such stakes as he had, and up and moved to Missoula because there were guiding opportunities and world-class fly fishing and hunting. Katy didn't fish or hunt, but she admired Jack and shared his spirit of adventure. By December she had found a job with the YMCA that seemed promising, a roommate, and a place to live. We visited her and Jack at Christmas, took pictures of the ski slopes and frozen lakes, climbed the trail to the "Big M" on Mount Sentinel overlooking the university, and returned to Memphis thinking all was well.

It was not. The winter nights were long and the days were short in the valley at that latitude. Katy had no friends other than Jack and her roommate. She did not ski. It was too cold for Ultimate. Her apartment was a bit of a dump. She did not have a car and tried to ride a bike through the ice and slush to work and back in the darkness. And the indoor job with a low-key nonprofit agency did not suit her. The only thing worse than too much to do is not enough to do. It was a perfect storm for depression, and it hit her hard within a few weeks.

She was suicidal. I shudder when I remember our long-distance phone conversations about how to buy a used car and make the best of a job until spring came and something better came along and her mother and I could get ourselves back out there. Somehow she forced herself to put a few things in a backpack, write farewell letters to her employer and her roommate, and get on a plane for Memphis. I found her alone in the house in the dark that night when I returned by early by chance from a tennis tournament.

"It's me, Katy. I came home." She was numb and I was terrified. She told me the raw details and tumbled into bed with our wiener dog for a day.

When she emerged from her shell a few days later, she saw a minister friend. Then another minister friend. My own oddball career as a newsman, freelance writer and columnist was a singular job path that offered little opportunity for her. She tried working as Jenny's painting assistant. We took long walks. We bought a used car together. My sister Ann wrote to her about her own post-college blues. None of this seemed to do much good, so we found a young therapist who made a connection, and by spring Katy was ready to return to Missoula and fight what I would later call the lion on her own terms, without antidepressants or more therapy.

She took a job with a group home for neglected and abused children, staying overnight with them and accompanying them to school for the whole day in case she had to wrestle them to the ground when they freaked out. She got a new apartment closer to Jack and the university and a new set of roommates. Her used car worked most of the time. The Ultimate Frisbee crowd realized what an ace she was and welcomed her to their ranks of wild hair and beards, wild costumes, and weekend road trips to Idaho, Oregon, Utah, and Canada. They probably saved her life.

Later that year she took over a friend's job that better suited her creative talents with an after-school program called Flagship at Hawthorne Elementary School. She was back in her element, getting outside, and working with kids and colleagues who loved her.

She had found her soul if not her career calling, at least not the kind they prepare you for in college. There was something inside her that drove her faster and farther than other people while making them feel good at the same time. So she took up cross-country skiing and long-distance biking, a Missoula specialty, and made regular trips to Yellowstone National Park and the nearby national forests. She met Dylan, a really good guy who loved the outdoors, and after a while they moved into a nice rental house together. Life was good.

Montana felt like our now-and-future summer home when we came to Missoula or Flathead Lake an hour north of it for summer vacations. Katy and Jack were in the same town. Their friends knew us now. We could rent a cabin on the lake and a boat to Wild Horse Island, climb hills to escape the harsh and fitful concerns of our lives, share picnic lunches with the wild goats, swim in gin-clear water, drink coffee on the dock at sunrise and wine on the bluff at sunset, take the annual year-end holiday picture.

Most important to all of us, we could be together as a family again.

6: Biking Across America, 2014:
"I'm having the freaking time of my life!"

"A journey is a person in itself; no two are alike. And all plans, safeguards, policing and coercion are fruitless. We find after years of struggle that we do not take a trip; a trip takes us."

—John Steinbeck on a card in Katy's room

"So many times her spirit for adventure fed my already high spirit. We had a ride date out of Carrizozo New Mexico and we decided we would first stop at Valley of the Fires Recreation Area where there was an interpretive walkway through a lava flow. We were equally competitive so we had to be the first to ride the path, which bikes were not supposed to be on. I remember feeling so alive when we stopped to take in the view of the desert, struggling up hills, a classic gas station stop, crossing the Rio Grande, the pool at the host location, and ginger beers at a dive bar...Katy will always ride on."

—Rose Matthews, Honolulu

"Katy B was an outlaw, wild, courageous and daring. Seeking adventure was second nature. She was curious and unapologetic about how she lived and loved life. She was so intent in conversation and really cared about what you had to say. That was really important for a lot of us, being at crossroads of thinking about what the future could hold while also having no clue how to begin. Katy B was a lighthouse for those of us lost at sea to find out way to solid ground. We

were all better for knowing Katy."

—Kelsey, Bike and Build 2014

"Katy was the lunch spot queen."

—Kristen Ewing, Pie Town, New Mexico, Bike and Build 2014

* * *

Biking was where Katy found peace. Adventure was her drug. Camaraderie was her salvation. Leading 32 young people on a cross-country bike trip of 3,993 miles in 75 days was a way to keep the lion at bay. Plan, pedal, eat, laugh, follow the white line on the highway, repeat.

I was not thrilled when Katy told Jenny and me that she had decided to bike across America in the summer of 2014. Katy was a risk taker. I am a risk avoider. Katy embraced challenges. I calculate ways to manage them. I rode the brakes on the downhills. Katy pedaled and soared.

I believe she got the idea from Adventure Cycling, which has its headquarters in Missoula a block from where Katy lived for two years. The office is decorated with vintage bikes and snapshots of cross-country cyclists who stopped in, including zanies on unicycles, tandems, clunky one-speeds, or towing small children behind them. The first time she brought it up was in a phone call when she suggested we could join her, taking turns riding with her or driving the car or SAG wagon (support and gear). I thought this was ridiculous, and told her so. Jenny was 58, with short legs and didn't even own a bike. I was 65 with bad knees and had never biked more than 70 miles in one day. She took that as a "no way" and discovered an outfit called Bike and Build.

I was still skeptical. It would interrupt her career. It would separate her from Dylan for 75 days. I was not a fan of crowd-sourced funding to raise the required $4,500 in pledges because I thought the cause of affordable housing would be seen as camouflage for personal expenses for a summer trip. (I was wrong about this; several Bike and Build alumni, including Katy, found careers in affordable housing and service jobs.) Most of all, I thought it was dangerous to bike 3,993 miles on roads meant for trucks and cars and motorcycles going 65 miles an hour. You could do everything right, take all the precautions, and still get killed. If the odds of an accident were 1 in 100, then someone was more likely than not to be killed or seriously injured. Every morning when I checked my email or answered the phone that summer I was afraid there would be bad news.

(A Bike and Build rider was killed in an accident in 2015, and another in 2016. After visiting the memorial site of the 2016 fatality in Idaho Falls, Katy wrote this on Facebook: "Let this be a reminder to everyone who drives a vehicle to be alert and watch for cyclists and to everyone who rides a bike to do everything within their control to minimize the inherent risks of cycling. The immediacy of any possible distraction – a text, a call, a picture, a music change, a bite of food – is never more important than the sacredness of the life of another human being. It could be you, me, one of your friends or family members.")

As I reread the blog entries Katy wrote that summer, I realize how wrong I was. And how right I was at the same time.

The riders dipped their bikes in the Atlantic Ocean at Portland Maine, and headed west. They would ride 50 to 100 miles (a "century") in a day for three or four days then rest a day or do a "build day" with a local group working on affordable housing. The route took them through 18 states in all.

Jenny and I met them in St. Louis to put faces on names we had read in her blog, *Cross-Country Katy*. We bought them pizza and cokes, wished them well, and watched them ride off in groups of two or three the next morning, followed by the SAG wagon driven by one of the leaders. I felt a little better about it all. In fact, I lived vicariously through Katy that summer. I remembered towns and national parks I had visited on family vacations in a station wagon 50 years ago. Part of me wished I was with them. We flew to California, rented a car in Oakland, and drove down the coast to Santa Barbara where they rode into town, gathered in a park, picked up flags of the states they has passed through, and triumphantly charged into the Pacific. It was thrilling and I wept.

From Cross-Country Katy, Summer of 2014

Maine: Where do I even start to describe the past week? I don't think my words can sum up the whirlwind that has been rider orientation and the first several days of this journey, so I'll keep it brief and let pictures do the talking. Our group quickly latched on to one another during two days of rider orientation, which involved icebreakers, presentations, trailer-painting, a shakedown ride, and a birthday celebration on day two for one of the riders.

I'm blown away at how quickly we've become so close, and how much I adore and care about the 32 other people I'll be with all summer. On the last day of orientation we had our first build day with Habitat for Humanity of Greater Portland. We worked on two different homes on the same lot and completed a TON of work in one day – roofing, insulation, painting and all sorts of other build terms I'm not quite familiar with yet. I did learn that the insulation techniques that Habitat uses can help cut annual energy costs by up to 2/3 of the average (which can translate into several thousand dollars). I also spent a fair amount of time on a ladder, hanging out of windows, and up and down scaffolding, which greatly appealed to my inner monkey. The local news station came and put together a piece for the nightly news,

Then on Friday we experienced the moment we had been waiting for for so long (6+ months!) – the wheel dip ceremony in the Atlantic

Ocean and the official start of our trip. We had a short ride from the church we stayed at down to the beach, and a few riders took a slight detour and added on some "bonus miles" as we like to call it. We have quickly come to find that getting lost and making wrong turns is always bound to happen and is nothing to sweat. Once everyone arrived, we lined up to dip our back tires in the water before taking off (with a lot of picture-taking and chanting in between). It's hard to believe that we'll be doing the same thing with our front wheels in the Pacific by the end of the summer.

From Portland we made our way to Kittery along winding coastal Maine roads and a shaded gravel trail. Any time my group made a wrong turn, we ended up somewhere awesome – a rocky beach with a view, a worn-down boat dock/shack covered in bouys, etc. We tacked on 5-10 bonus miles that day and arrived at the host site happier than ever. I've been blown away by the hospitality of the hosts (mostly churches and schools) that we stay with. There are personalized signs, welcoming parties, homemade meals, snacks and more awaiting our arrival. The locals have been incredibly hospitable and interested in our adventure, and I've already had countless conversations with people who felt like a good friend by the time we left the next morning. We even had a spontaneous drum/dance circle in a gazebo in the middle of a park in downtown Fitchburg, MA that was maybe my favorite moment of the trip thus far (so many to choose from!!).

Here's a few more pictures from this first week. I don't think I'll have much time to blog, but I hope I can continue posting pictures and brief updates/descriptions of how the trip has been going. I sent out my first 10 donor postcards yesterday, so be on the lookout for those! In a nutshell, I'm having the freaking time of my life!

"Best Worst Day Ever"

Indiana: Our last ride in Indiana was perhaps the most memorable of the trip thus far. It was a 95 mile day to Salem, IL, and I was riding sweep (last back) with my buddy Kelsey. The day was a series of ups and downs that included sweeping a couple riders who needed to ride in the van due to illness/injury, jumping on hay bales, riding my 1000th mile of the trip, crossing our first time zone, and eventually catching up to a group of riders who experienced the misfortune of almost 10 flat tires in a day. Every time they flatted out we stopped to help and admire the view of the endless roadside cornfields. Our progress was painfully slow, as we would make it no more than a couple miles before the next flat.

By the time we reached second lunch (we have two lunches on 90+ mile days), it was already 4 p.m.. We still had almost 25 miles to go and groups ahead reported a "wicked" storm approaching. As we finished gorging ourselves with snacks, the dark clouds loomed overhead and we decided to try to make it as far as we could before seeking shelter. As we pedaled out of the parking lot and over the adjacent bridge crossing the state line into Illinois, the storm did its best to keep us in Indiana. I could barely rotate my pedals to get up and over the bridge as the wind picked up and the rain began. On the other side of the bridge one of my riding partners, Lucas, and I stopped just long enough to take a picture in front of the state sign. We cackled hysterically while getting drenched in our attempt to document the moment.

About a hundred feet away our group had taken shelter in an abandoned building that appeared to be covered in bullet holes. After waiting out the storm for another 45 minutes, we decided to forego the offer to be picked up by the van and finish the ride. A few miles in we found ourselves riding along a winding country road with a pink sunset over a lake to our left and the thunderclouds moving away from us to the right. The lighting was perfect and everything sparkled with moisture from the storm. That's when we realized we had made a wrong turn and gone several miles in the wrong direction. On the way back to our route, Chris got another flat. It was almost 7 p.m. and we had been on the road for a full 12 hours with 15 miles left to go. Out of tubes and unsure if the bikes would hold up, we decided to call it quits and have the van come pick us up. It wasn't how we envisioned our day ending, but the group morale was high up to the very end.

We coined it the "best worst day ever" to encapsulate the highs and lows of the days and the fact that there are no bad days on Bike & Build.

California: I slacked off on my blogging duties during the last two... err...three...weeks of the trip. I chalk it up to "living in the moment" like my dad encouraged me to at the start of the trip. I was trying to savor every last minute of the experience instead of sitting in front of a screen. And I didn't have good internet. And I was tired. And the dog ate my iPad. Ok, you get the point. Nevertheless, I want to do some retro-blogging mostly for selfish reasons, so that I can have this blog to look back on and jog my memory of the trip of a lifetime. So here's a play-by-by of the last three weeks of the trip, and once I've had the time to settle down and wrap my brain around all of this, maybe I'll even write up some final thoughts filled with all kinds of inspiration and life-changing realizations.

Arizona Week 2

Sedona to Flagstaff: Having passed through Sedona before, I knew it would be a scenic ride, albeit a long one (90 miles). I was a little bummed to be driving the van that day, but the view through the window wasn't half bad. As we approached Sedona, dark clouds loomed beyond the red rocks, quickly engulfing the town and casting an eerie shadow on the rock formations. By the time I reached the church with the van and trailer, a full-on storm had commenced, with thick sheets of rain and hail. What did our group do? They ran outside half naked and proceeded to take a "rain shower" while hollering like a bunch of bandits. Check out this time lapse video of the storm rolling in.

Flagstaff was easily one of my favorite towns of the trip, as it reminded me a lot of Missoula with it's down-to-earth college town feel and abundance of outdoor recreation opportunities. I was glad we had a build day there to allow some extra time to explore the city. Our build day with the local Habitat chapter split us into several groups to complete various service projects around town, some building-related and some not. My crew completed our project at a new home construction site well before lunch, so we checked out some local shops and then joined forces with another crew in the afternoon to split firewood. I happily added the wood-splitter (vertical and horizontal varieties) to my power tool repertoire.

Grand Canyon: Biking to the Grand Canyon was one of those surreal moments on the trip where I had to take a step back and think, "Wow, we are really doing this!". The majority of the people in our group had never been to the Grand Canyon, so the anticipation was high. From the moment we arrived at the gateway town to the south rim entrance of the park, we were surrounded by international tourists, many of whom found our matching Bike & Build attire picture-worthy. We quickly made a game out of guessing the different languages and accents we heard around us. Once we settled into the campground we made our way to the canyon for first views and the mandatory photo shoot. Holding a bike above your head on the edge of the canyon was more nerve-wracking than the smile on the my face might suggest. Over the course of the next two days,

I witnessed two sunsets and a sunrise over the canyon and hiked six miles down into the canyon (I try to forget the six miles back up it). We had campfires and star-gazing sessions to cap off our first two nights camping together and miraculously left the campground without a single noise complaint.

Santa Barbara: I remember going to bed after midnight the night before our ride into Santa Barbara thinking I'd never fall asleep. Not because I was sleeping on a church pew – I'd grown quite accustomed to that – but because I was so amped for what the next day would bring. I managed to get a few hours of sleep in, waking up before my alarm in the same frenzied state I'd fallen asleep in. This was it. The day I'd dreamed of for nearly nine months.

Today we were going to put on our jerseys, mount our bikes, and ride to the Pacific Ocean. 75 days before, we had done the same, only leaving the Atlantic. We had ridden our bikes across the entire U.S. We decided to make a "leader sandwich", so Jeff and Emily led the pack while Becca and I brought up the rear as sweep. We only had 40 miles to ride to Santa Barbara, and we made it to the coast in Ventura within the first 15. That first glimpse of the Pacific is a moment that will be forever etched in my memory. I remember yelling and lifting our bikes up and telling every stranger who passed by us "WE BIKED HERE", as if expecting them to acknowledge or even remotely understand what that meant to us.

We excitedly biked along the coast, stopping reluctantly for a group with a flat…then I got a flat…then Dan got a flat. Our eagerness to get to the group's meeting spot couldn't be stifled. Finally we rolled into the Santa Barbara cemetery, where our 30 teammates chanted "SWEEP, SWEEP, SWEEP" as we entered the gates. With our whole crew accounted for, we regrouped and rode en masse along the streets of Santa Barbara for the final mile, cheering, chanting and cow-belling the whole way. I can't imagine what we looked like to the cars and people we passed. Once we arrived at the beach, we had to resist the urges to run immediately into the ocean or into the arms of friends and family so that we could all run into the Pacific as a unified group. With the American flag and a flag from each of the 18 states we passed through, we charged the beach then stormed into the ocean.

The party that ensued was a blur of champagne and ocean spray, hugs and cheers amidst a wave pool that tried to push us apart every time we came together to form a huddle. We made it, all 33 of us, from Maine to Santa Barbara.

7: Getting people to do stuff. For free.

In May of 2016, Katy gave this speech at the Flathead Valley Community College Student Leadership Awards Ceremony. She called it "Lessons Learned on a Cross-Country Bike Trip."

* * *

Good morning student leaders, faculty, family and friends. You might be wondering what qualifies me to serve as your guest speaker today. Well if you were hoping for a six-figured CEO, a powerful political figure, a local celebrity or some otherwise impressive big shot with a wall full of awards and accolades – I'm sorry to disappoint you. If it wasn't for this speaking occasion I'd probably be wearing jeans and a hoodie, and this morning my breakfast consisted of the last remaining spoonful of peanut butter in my pantry. But if you are hoping to hear from someone who is rich in life experiences, powerful in mind and spirit, and well-adored by a fan club that consists of my mom and dad, then hopefully I have something to offer you today.

A little bit about me. I grew up in Memphis, Tennessee, so if my drawl or my "y'all" sneak in here, then 'bless yer heart', as my southern mama would say. I spent my college years in North Carolina at a small liberal arts school called Elon University, where my formal degree was in Corporate Communications with unofficial minors in ultimate Frisbee, pulling all-nighters, intramural ping-pong and themed costume parties. In my four years at Elon I graduated as part of the Honors program, captained my club sports team, worked as a campus tour guide and student ambassador, volunteered with Katrina relief efforts on a spring break service trip, spent a semester studying abroad in Italy, orchestrated a campus-wide substance abuse prevention campaign, completed an internship with a local business devoted to Corporate Social Responsibility and published a two-year undergraduate research project on the impact of online social networks on non-profit organizations. I was a total nerd, but I managed to come out of those four years a more well-rounded, grounded person.

After college I stumbled upon Montana, and so began a love affair with the mountains, rivers and wild places of this state that has lasted for the last six years – yes, we are in a long-term relationship and it is Facebook official. I spent my first four years in Montana living in Missoula and working and volunteering for various youth-serving organizations including the YMCA, Partnership for Children, the YWCA and the Flagship Program. In my three years with the Flagship Program I served as the program coordinator at an elementary school, designing and overseeing roughly 50 enrichment-based after school and summer programs each year, serving 300 students annually, and managing an army of around 100 volunteers, most of which were college students. I led efforts to build a school garden, established an annual bike-to-school and bike safety event, and held the state's first ever elementary school-based sports program for students with and without intellectual disabilities through a partnership with the Special Olympics Project Unify program.

So why am I telling you all of this about myself? This is _your_ awards ceremony, this should be about <u>YOU</u>. Well, for one, I was told I had 20-25 minutes to fill, which is a long time, so I have to flesh this thing out somehow. And second, it's been the collection of all of these experiences that has helped me develop the leadership skills and philosophy that I have today along with instilling in me the deep-seeded values of volunteerism and community engagement.

The culmination of all of these experiences I had in my so-called formative years and early 20s were put to the ultimate leadership test during the summer of 2014 when I co-led a service-oriented cross-country cycling trip for an organization called Bike & Build. This is the leadership experience I want to focus on today and share with you five important lessons I learned about what it means to be a good leader.

A good leader takes risks and aims high. Before my summer with Bike & Build I had mostly ridden on rusty old hand-me-downs that clicked and clacked like an old typewriter. I had never ridden more than 50 miles in a day. I had never ridden long distances for more than two days consecutively. I had never changed a flat tire, but this one time my friend showed me and this other time I watched a YouTube video, so I said that I could. I was a fair-weather biker. So was I ready to lead a 4,000 mile bike ride across the country? You bet. It's not about your qualifications, it's about your determination. *Don't* play it safe. Take risks. Aim high.

A good leader has an unwavering positive attitude. I want to tell you a little story about what I call "The Best Worst Day Ever."...As a good leader, you must have an unwavering positive attitude in the face of uncertainty, obstacles and problems that can and will inevitably arise.

A good leader knows when to take a back seat. The cowboy Will Rogers once said, "Never miss a good chance to shut up." As a good leader, you have to know when to take the wheel and drive and when to sit in the back seat and keep your mouth shut.

A good leader owns up to their mistakes. On a "century" ride in Arizona, our leader team miscalculated the weather and road conditions and the morale of our fellow riders. In short, we messed up. We made a mistake, and we owned up to it, probably not as well as we could have in the moment, but our team forgave us and ultimately appreciated the vulnerability we showed in that apology. So don't be afraid to make mistakes. In fact, I encourage you to make them, but the key is that you own up to them and learn from them. Fail, fail, fail again. You might even find that your perceived failures are rife with hidden lessons that you're meant to learn all along.

A good leader builds relationships and community. As a good leader, you have to take the time to get to know the people you're leading on a personal level as often as you can. Listen, ask questions, go out of your way to do something nice for someone, _show_ them that you truly care, celebrate their successes, comfort them in the hard times, make them laugh, _tell_ people out loud how much you value and appreciate them.

Now that I can safely say we've digested the leadership topic, I'd like to move on to the importance of volunteerism and community engagement. I work with and recruit volunteers for a living. It's what I do. If there's one thing I'm an expert at, it's getting people to do stuff. For free. No, volunteering is about a lot more than that. Volunteering strikes a deep chord in the melody of life, satisfying innate human desires to feel meaningful, fulfilled, connected and loving towards our fellow humans. Your time as a human being on this planet is the fastest depleting natural resource in the world. It's not oil, or gas, or coal or Miley Cyrus's innocence – it's your time. So when you offer your time to a cause, an organization, another person, it is so valuable. It is truly a gift.

So find out what sets you on fire and go do it. What makes your heart pound, your mind race with ideas, your creativity blossom? Be curious, explore what makes you tick, and if you don't know what that is right now, that's ok too. Just be curious and keep exploring and giving back. And remember this little haiku – you know, 5-7-5 poetry.

"To challenge yourself is to empower others for the greater good" – those 17 syllables sum up my philosophy of leadership better than anything else I can say. "To challenge yourself is to empower others for the greater good."

If not you, then who? If not now, then when? You can do it. We can do it. Go get 'em, team. Thank you.

8: Build Days, Golden Days, and the Night Train

"I participated in a build in Montana in September of 2016. Katy not only kept us organized but really shared her enthusiasm for Habitat and Montana. We both shared the passion for the difference a permanent home made in the life of a child. Katy was all about the kids. I knew instantly when Katy was on the site as a swarm of kids would go running to her."

—Laura Brown, Bristow

"I am an old woman (60!) and as my time runs out I constantly question how we know we have made a difference on this earth. I realize that it is partly based on the lives we touch and whether people retain memories of us. Katy touched my heart and so many others by the wonderful life she lived. It is difficult to understand why she should be taken at such a young age. The only solace is that she truly will be remembered by me and countless others."

—Jane Bachmann, Chicago

"We've done Habitat since 2008 and never encountered a spirit that touched us like hers did. Her vitality, joy, energy, inclusiveness and compassion were unparalleled. She was a delight to all of us Care-a-Vanners."

—Jo Ann Safranek, Yuma

"First, I miss you. You did so many kind things for Genia and I. You were the friend at work who reached out and jumped in to help me when I first learned my wife was ill. And then as our life got crazy you continued to be there for us, covering for me at the build site, sending home soup with me, tuning up our bikes in the hope that Genia would feel well enough to get out and peddle a bit. The greatness you had was evident in your work. As I reflect on my Habitat life, so many of the accomplishments at the build site have your involvement in them. As emotionally difficult as it has been since you left, progress on the build site needed to continue. The goal was to have the Davidson's home ready for final inspection by December 31st, satisfying a requirement to receive the grant that had been arranged on that home. With help from our volunteers, we accomplished that goal. I could not have been more pleased and proud. Thank you for your work in setting this up for me."

—Steve Tartaglino, construction site supervisor in Kalispell, in a "letter to Katy" after her death.

"Build Days", sung by Katy playing the ukulele to the tune of "My Girl"

I've got rock work, on a cloudy day
Whichever tape I use I'm still an inch away
I bet Steve will say you better make it fit the right way
Build days, talkin' 'bout build days, build days
I've got so much back pain from all this scaffolding
I've got a piece of shingle, that's really baffling
(Chorus)
I don't need no help and I'm not gonna quit
I just really need that last piece of drywall to fit
(Chorus)
I've got so much warmth deep in my heart
Because the Care-a-Vanners make building an art
I bet Steve will say you did a really good job today
Build days, talkin' bout build days, build days.

* * *

After Katy finished the cross country bike trip in the summer of 2014 she moved in with Dylan in a house in Whitefish. It was a small wooden two-story house with an overgrown front yard, a covered driveway for his fishing boat, and a backyard that sloped down to the Flathead River. Riparian, he called it. She had to leave a job she liked in Missoula and find a new one in Whitefish. She took a part-time job working at an elementary school doing after-school activities, and another part-time job with Habitat for Humanity of Flathead Valley, a fulfillment of her promise made through Bike and Build.

They took a raft trip down the Salmon River in Idaho with friends, and everything seemed to be all right. They skied together in the winter at Big Mountain a few miles away, and could see the mountains in the morning light from their north-facing bedroom window. Not incidentally, I noted, Katy also traveled to a lot of weddings, as one after another of her old friends from high school and college and Missoula got married.

It was a mild winter that year of transition, and Habitat was able to build nearly every week, which kept Katy busy recruiting volunteers and donations. We visited them in April and stayed at the house for a week. Jenny painted a fish picture for the living room, painted the staircase and kitchen, and put up new curtains. I helped clean up the backyard and haul trash to the dump. We built rough steps through the riparian to the river and a new fire pit from the old bricks. Friends came over for a cookout and a night of "fire pit frivolity".

We worked at a Habitat build site and were assigned to painting, which is the job given to newbies without any building skills. We saw Katy interact with the volunteers and met the site boss, Steve. She was proud of us for coming out, and we felt good about ourselves for being there. We came back to Memphis expecting a good summer and possibly a wedding. We never talked about that with them though. That was their business, not ours.

Late that summer Katy took another long bike trip, "Drift West," 900 miles in three weeks through the Pacific Northwest. She clinched the leadership job with an application that included a hand-drawn map of the places they would go. Again, I worried about the narrow roads shared with distracted drivers and logging trucks, the separation from the man she loved, and the time away from her job. This did not square with the picture of fire-pit frivolity. I felt in my gut that something was missing, that she fighting against something. The lion maybe.

That October I had a small stroke that put me in the hospital for a night. A series of CT scans and MRIs showed blockage of the vertebral artery that was the likely cause of my sudden inability to walk a straight line or keep my balance. Katy called that weekend, but then we did not hear from her again for nearly a month. I sensed that something was wrong. The email came at the end of the month. She and her guy had decided to end it. She was heartbroken. She did not want to talk about what happened or why and asked that we not ask about it. She was moving in with two friends, Tristan and Tracy, in their house in Whitefish. She assured us she would get through it. Winter was coming on.

She came to Memphis two days before Christmas, arriving early enough to join our closest neighbors for a ping-pong party at our house. Ping pong was one of Katy's favorite family events, and she was her old self as we played doubles and a family favorite called Around the World and awarded a silly prize to the winner. But the next day, Christmas Eve, she was deep in a funk. We took a walk down by the river and she barely spoke the whole time. She forced a smile for family pictures on the bluff steps painted with the logo of the Memphis Grizzlies but her heart wasn't in it.

On Christmas morning, she rallied and seemed to enjoy opening presents. But the sadness came out again when we talked about her plans for January. She had signed on with Adventure Cycling to lead a two-week trip through the Florida Keys. They would fly her there and pay to ship her a new bike, but it meant that she was basically unemployed again. She had also indicated that she would lead another cross-country trip for Adventure Cycling in the summer with only a handful of other riders and no SAG wagon.

In a long tearful talk in our living room, I told her to take the Florida trip and cancel the summer trip even if she had to reimburse Adventure Cycling. Go back to work. Habitat is a good organization. You can grow there and have a career. DO NOT under any circumstances take another cross-country ride. It was the most forceful I had ever been with her, and I think it had an impact. The Florida trip was a downer with strong winds, cold days, and an older clientele that did not bond like the Bike and Build gang. As Katy described it in her journal, "It was 12 days filled with guilt, shame, and anxiety. I felt bad about deceiving the group, which made me anxious, depressed, and withdrawn. I had a hard time connecting with people."

She returned to Whitefish and vowed to move forward with a regimen of exercise, reading, writing, Habitat work, and therapy sessions with a counselor. She hand wrote and signed a "contract" with herself to "LET GO of the past and EMBRACE the future, giving it my best effort and striving to be the beautiful, wonderful, complex person that I am." She took the train to Portland to see her best friend Lindsay, whose marriage had ended in divorce a year earlier.

"She was still so broken, confused, and somewhat beating herself up from the breakup and was not her upbeat self," Lindsay later wrote. "But she did what she always did and rose to the occasion. She also was realizing that she didn't want to continue leading bike trips at this time. It seemed to really sadden her that she didn't have the desire to do it anymore. She swung on this insane rope swing on a hike that made me unbelievably nervous, but it's another picture of her just wanting to feel alive."

Thanks in part to another early spring, things started looking up. Katy joined a young professionals group. Habitat sent her to a Colorado convention, made her full-time with benefits, and gave her a raise. She ran a benefit 5K wearing a tool belt and a hard had. Any day she could put on a costume was a good day. Using her balky manual typewriter, she wrote a brilliant 2500-word narrative, "The First Bicycle Tour of the Glacier National Park," in the archaic style of "wheelman" W. O. Owen, the first cyclist to ride into Yellowstone National Park in 1883: "Our disbelief in the sheer wildness of our surroundings was counteracted only by the undeniable authenticity of the experience as a whole."

And she found a new place to live, as a renter/caretaker for a Whitefish woman who was planning to be away for six months and was willing to cut the rent to $500 a month for the right renter. The house was modern, well furnished, and had a garden and backyard deck. It was half a mile from a state park on Whitefish Lake. It was perfect, or so it seemed. She was getting the breaks. Her luck had changed.

It was a golden summer. We had a family reunion in June with Jack and my sister and brother-in -law at their home in Berkeley. We borrowed their convertible for a drive up the coast to Muir Woods where we took a family picture in front of a giant tree that was so perfect that Jenny and I proudly put it out on social media.

I flew to Whitefish for another week with Katy. Each morning she made me a smoothie then dropped me off at "day care" at the build site. In the evenings we biked, baked rhubarb pies, made up a song called "More Avocado, That's My Motto", and swam in the lakes. The "young seniors" came back like seasonal birds in their motor homes to work at the Habitat houses. Katy loved their enthusiasm, skills, big hearts, and joshing, and they loved her for her grace, humor, and ability to give as good as she got. She coined the word "Habitatitis" for their contagious enthusiasm. I was so proud of her when she gathered everyone together at the morning meeting, thanked the sponsors and volunteers, told a joke or made up a song, and put them to work.

Communications, I realized, was exactly the business she belonged in.

Not only did she have motivational skills and the heart of a lion in the face of danger, she had a remarkable ability to defuse tension. One afternoon when I was staying with her, there was a furious banging on the door of the condo. Katy opened the door and was confronted by a hysterical young woman demanding to know the whereabouts of Katy's landlord. Clearly she had violence and vengeance on her mind. Had she not seen me in the living room, I believe she would have forced her way into the house and torn apart anything and anyone in her path. Katy calmly spoke to her, refused to disclose the whereabouts of the landlord, and firmly told the woman to leave. Something about her tone and demeanor convinced the crazy woman to back down, and she got into her car and sped away, giving us the finger and throwing something out the window. I took it to be a weapon, but fortunately it was not. Katy called the police and the landlord and went on about her day. Had I answered the door, there is no doubt in my mind that I would have lost my temper, shouted at the hell bitch, and provoked a fight.

Jenny and I flew back out to Whitefish in August. We spent three days working on drywall at a build site with some families with kids who were about Katy's age. By the third day we were ahead of schedule, so Katy arranged an Amtrak train trip at sunrise for us from Whitefish through Glacier National Park to East Glacier with seats in the observation car. She met us in her car at the train station and drove us to a lake for a boat ride and a hike, then back home over Logan Pass on the famous Going to the Sun Road and along Lake McDonald at sunset. It was a classic Katy bucket-list day. We walked down to the train tracks near her house that night, placed pennies and nickels on the rails so the wheels would flatten them into souvenirs, and waited in darkness for the Empire Builder to come roaring through the valley on its nightly run to the West Coast. It was indescribably beautiful, perfect, and now, in memory, heartbreaking.

I thought of the writer Bruce Catton's haunting metaphor about death as the night train: "And there is the headlight, shining far down the track, glinting off the steel rails that, like all parallel lines, will meet in infinity, which after all is where this train is going."

We didn't know it would stop for us so soon.

9: December 9, 2016: One Month After

This is the part where I blame my parents and myself.

The nostalgic version of the 1950s as households of fathers who knew best and mothers who wore pumps and dresses with their aprons in the kitchen was mostly a fantasy, of course.

My father had depression most of his adult life, hated his father for years for wanting him to be something he could not, and had a nervous breakdown and lost his job when he was 50 years old and I was in college.

My mother had a first-class mind, a degree in English from Northwestern, a master's degree in Library Science from Michigan and lived in a self-imposed prison of claustrophobia and a society-imposed one of suburban conformity and motherhood a generation before Women's Liberation. How many career opportunities she missed I do not know for sure, but I refused to let her be the librarian at my high school because the duties included presiding over study hall where all sorts of shenanigans went on. Her name was Marion, and I knew my classmates would make fun of Marion the Librarian, like in the musical *The Music Man*, when she made them get back in their seats and be quiet until the bell rang. So she took a non-job as a "reference librarian" at a packaging company on the other side of Grand Rapids doing nothing much useful to herself or anyone else.

When Dad had his breakdown in Michigan in 1968 I was taking summer school classes in California and got the news in a telephone call from Mother.

"Your father has had a nervous breakdown and lost his job. Don't come home. Finish your classes. It's OK. Your sister and I are here."

Too self-absorbed to grasp the magnitude of this event, I stayed where I was. When I got home, Dad coaxed me into a long walk with him, told me the story, put a brave face on things, and shared his fantasy of moving to northern Michigan and opening a motel near Lake Michigan where he grew up. I said that sounded like a good idea. This pouring-your-heart-out business was new to both of us. In the giddy aftermath of the breakdown and the tentative first steps on recovery road, Dad bought a tandem bicycle, which he promptly stored in the basement. He might as well have bought a pair of Harley Davidsons. Mother never rode a bike, never got on an airplane until after she was diagnosed with terminal cancer in 1971, and was terrified of driving a car more than six blocks. Her claustrophobia kicked in near tunnels, and she once made Dad make a U-turn on a divided highway when we approached a tunnel near Knoxville that was not marked on the infallible AAA Trip Map.

A few years before he died of cancer in 2001, Dad shared with me his army papers and executive psychological analysis with its highs and lows and warning signs. He annotated it with this note. "I'm convinced it's very hard for people to change their basic personalities. Of paramount importance to me, then as now, was success in marriage, family, and home. I think I did achieve those goals."

I think Dad was right. Personality is an ever-shifting balance between self-belief and self-doubt. Motivational exercises and life events can shift the balance somewhat, sometimes. For better and worse, this was the baggage I inherited and passed along, with my own contributions, to my children.

When I had my own near meltdown as my marriage ended in

divorce I was 29 years old, the same age as Katy when she took her life. I had a brief period of what medical people call suicidal ideation while living alone through the coldest winter of the century in Wisconsin. That means you think about it but don't take any steps toward carrying it out. I survived on Old Style beer, one-night stands, racquetball, hours spent reading Gay Talese and John McPhee and the New Journalists, and a glimmer of hope derived from selling a few articles with my first bylines after changing careers. I spent $50 on a therapy session and did not go back. I went home to Michigan at Christmas and cried on my father's shoulder. Adrift in a meaningless job in Madison and literally frozen in place, I got into my Volkswagen in March when the temperature warmed up enough for the little heater to clear the windshield. My imperative: sell the house, keep the dog, get away, go South. I was lucky to land a job with UPI in Nashville. Suddenly I was a bonafide newsman. I got transferred to Jackson, Mississippi, met Jenny by chance on a tennis court, and life got better.

No matter how much I read, I cannot convince myself that depression is a disease, not a product of circumstance. My depression, if that it was, was not as severe as Katy's. My life changed because of a combination of desperation, luck, chance, racquetball, and the soothing sound of the Doobie Brothers singing "What A Fool Believes" on the radio as I drove into the warm temperatures and blooming forsythia of spring in Nashville.

I never saw my starter wife again and did not return to Madison for 30 years. I never sat down with my children to talk about my first marriage. There was always next year. Some other time. There were no children from it so no harm no foul. They found out about it when they were teenagers looking through an old photo album. The unspoken message, I suppose, was that intimate relationships are your own business. If you want to talk about them, fine. If not, fine. When and if you get married is up to you. Work it out.

I told Katy all of this after her breakdown after she moved to Missoula in 2010. She saved her life that winter by flying home unannounced instead of jumping off a bridge into the Clark Fork River. She took a cab from the airport to our house and sat in the freezing cold garage until I came home.

Jenny and I were shocked, grateful, relieved, and confused as to what to do next. My father-daughter talk a couple of weeks later was similar to the one I had with my father in 1968. Whether it did any good or not, I can't say for sure. We urged Katy to see a therapist, and discussed with her the possible benefits of taking anti-depressants. Aided by the therapy sessions, two months later Katy moved back to Missoula and resumed the battle against depression on her own terms, with renewed determination and without psychiatry or drugs. She faced down that real mountain lion a well as the one inside her.

But I knew it was there, knew that she knew it was there, knew that it could and probably would come back, and that when it did I would not be of much help. When your children grow up and live thousands of miles away and you see them only a few times a year it is natural, I suppose, to go into denial. Katy and I were both aware of this gulf and it hurt us more than anyone knew. I was as uptight as she was open and uninhibited.

Years after my father overcame his hatred of his father and made his peace, he told me the movie that expressed his regrets was "I Never Sang for my Father" with Gene Hackman and Melvin Douglass. One way I divide people is those who dance and those who do not dance. I regret that I never danced with my daughter.

10: Christmas 2016

We made the three-hour drive down from Memphis to Jackson on the afternoon of Christmas Eve, talking only a little and listening to Norah Jones over and over singing about Pain and Peace and Flipside. It was raining when we left but clearing an hour later and sunny as we neared Jackson, with the golden hour glowing over the fields on the west side of the highway.

With a visit to Grandy in the nursing home on our schedule before we got to dinner at Dixie Gardens, we decided a snack was in order. A snack became dinner when we saw a sign for Piccadilly cafeteria and the lure of hot food and vegetables instead of a cheeseburger. The place was closing when we came in just after 5 and the help was taking the trays off the hot line. But they fed us anyway, baked chicken and green beans and carrot souffle for Jenny and baked catfish, carrot souffle and black-eyed peas and a roll for me. There were only a few other customers eating while the waitresses began vacuuming and clearing tables so they could get home for Christmas Eve. Carrot souffle is a holiday tradition for us thanks to Piccadilly, and really shouldn't count as a vegetable because they make it so sweet. But that's OK on Christmas Eve. A guy next to us thanked the server and handed her a $10 bill. Jenny did the same when we finished, paid our bill of $20.90 and got back in the car for the

45-minute drive to Hazlehurst. Dinner was out of the question now but that was fine because Kim and David had been up since dawn entertaining Kim's big family and their little kids.

The nursing home where Grandy has spent the last two years was lit up but no one was at the front desk when we got there with our potted plant and bag of cookies and cake. An attendant on smoke break beckoned us to a side entrance. A couple of residents in wheelchairs stared at us and nodded as we walked to #217, Janice Sanderson's room. It was empty. "She's smoking," Jenny said, and we walked down the long quiet, cheerless corridor of God's waiting room to the dimly lit outdoor porch where visitors are not supposed to go unless they key in a door code or are accompanied by staff. Grandy was sitting in a chair smoking a Kent, her "friend" Tammy at her side. We hugged her and made small talk for a few minutes before Jenny teared up and whispered a few words about Katy and our great sadness. Grandy nodded "I know." and held her hand.

That was my cue to get up and walk to the other end of the patio, and I broke down crying as I looked up into the blackness of the sky and the brightness of Venus in the western horizon and thought how my baby was billions of miles away, lost in the stars, and I would never see her, hear her, touch her again. I gave them another 20 minutes, then we said our goodbyes and left the way we came in, past a growing group of sad residents in their wheelchairs and lonesomeness and memory of who knows what. We had left the bag of cookies in Grandy's room. I had planned to pass them out Santa-style but was denied the self-gratifying satisfaction of virtue.

Kim and David were back in their room when we got to Dixie Gardens. The dogs, Bella the german shepherd and Bess the fluffy mess must have been back there too, so we let ourselves in. After a few minutes they came out and greeted us, opened up the leftovers. We picked over them, and looked at pictures of Kim's beautiful grandkids. They were dressed up in Indian costumes as Chief Fullabull and his tribe. That warm afternoon they had climbed up on the hay bales with the dogs and chased each other around, jumping from one to the next one and occasionally disappearing between them and then reappearing with a grin on their faces, as Katy had done this time last year. Somewhere we have the pictures. We talked about sleeping pills and breathing machines and sleep apnea and the usual concerns of young geezers and I went to bed before 9.

I forced myself to think of something besides Katy and got five or six hours of good sleep plus several naps without the violent dreams ambien can sometimes induce. First to bed was also first up. I went out to the patio, saw the sun coming up over the rye grass field across Dixie Garden road, and heard the tinkle of wind chimes hanging from the pecan tree, hoping there might be a Zen insight for me in there. William, the hired man, had pulled up earlier in his white pickup truck and was now firing up the tractor. He has turned the place into a beautiful farm, green and golden around the ponds, hay bales neatly stacked in the corrugated shed that stands where the rainbow barn once cheered us.

I walked down the hill by the tennis court to meet him.

"Good morning," he said. "Merry Christmas."

"Merry Christmas to you, and I guess it's like any other day for you," I offered.

"They got to be fed," he said of the cows, which were lowing if that is what you call it, just like they are supposed to do on Christmas even if they have a date with the slaughterhouse. "They cain't fend fer theyselves."

Off he went down the road to the cows, his hay bale of breakfast behind him. When he dropped it off, untied it, and spread the hay out he would turn around and do it again. And again. And again. Because that is what good people of character do.

Which was my Christmas story for this terrible year of 2016. You get out of bed. You put on your clothes. And you go out into the world and do whatever it is that you do, and try to make things a little bit better for yourself and others who can't fend for themselves. Then you get up the next day and do it again. And again the day after that.

Jenny is still sleeping, and God knows she needs it. When she gets up we will say goodbye to Kim and David and Dixie Gardens and drive down to our new home on the coast in Pass Christian. We plan to spend a lot of time there next year as we try to carry on with our lives without Katy but with the loving comfort of her big brother Jack, the best son, and our wonderful friends and family. Thank you to every one of you. Make someone laugh every day.

11: New Year's Day 2017: Photos and The Blue Urn

There are pictures of Katy in every room in our house, 27 in all, more if you count each one individually in the composites.

I know this because I obsessively counted them today. There are baby pictures, childhood pictures, graduation pictures, brother-sister pictures, father-daughter pictures, mother-daughter pictures, family pictures, holiday pictures, poster-size pictures, embossed wallet-size pictures, and the picture I use as the desktop background on my computer.

In addition to these there are two coffee-table books of pictures lovingly collected and annotated for us postmortem by her friends from Habitat for Humanity and Bike and Build. There are hundreds more on Facebook.

In every one of them Katy is smiling, laughing, or mugging for the camera.

The single exception, and I have obsessively searched for this too, is one I took on Christmas Eve 2015 on the Mississippi River bluff in Memphis. She is alone and has her back turned and is silhouetted against the river and bridge at sunset. She seems to be looking for someone or something.

These photos are not life stories, of course, they are more akin to highlight reels on ESPN or a family reunion or wedding album. How many times does the average person laugh in a day? Maybe 20? Maybe 50 if they are having a good day? Maybe once or twice or never if they are isolated and lonely? Only in snapshots do us cooperative types smile all the time.

Katy was definitely isolated and lonely, but almost nobody captured that in a picture. Or even took an unposed picture of her going about her business, which is one of the basic guidelines of my former trade, journalism. Two months after her death, I, however, laugh much more than I cry every day. Strange, isn't it?

Her ashes are in a blue urn on our side porch, next to some plants and candles and, of course, pictures. I go out there every day since her death and light a candle and write thank-you cards, read mail, or just sit there. Sometimes I talk to her before I blow out the candle.

Katy was cremated in Whitefish. Jack and my sister Ann handled the painful details with the funeral home while Jenny and I remained in Memphis. Jack brought the ashes home in the blue urn in a backpack he carried on to the plane. After he unpacked it, we put the urn on a table on the porch to get it out of the way but in view, and it has been there undisturbed ever since. Maybe some day we will scatter some ashes in Glacier National Park on Going to the Sun Road if that isn't illegal, but not soon. The porch is a good resting place, and it feels right.

The pictures are alright for now too, but I need more than that to honor Katy's memory. Pictures alone feel like denial. So I sit on the porch and go through her journals or sit at my desk and think about how much she fought and hurt and write notes for this book about the Katy who didn't always smile.

12: A Eulogy by Lindsay Morris

Katy,

When you came to Grahamwood in sixth grade wearing Umbros and an oversized t-shirt, I knew we were going to be good friends. However, I had no idea what we had ahead of us. Middle school was full of awkward moments. We began our competitive endeavors by seeing who could catch the most sour skittles in our mouths, started our periods and figured out how to use a tampon, and dressed up as Sweet N Low and Equal for Halloween. Seriously the worst costumes ever. I'm 90% positive it was your idea.

High school was definitely more enjoyable and slightly less awkward. We upped our competition game with ping pong, bowling, darts, speed scrabble, etc... You know, the normal things to be overly competitive about. Good thing you had terrible taste in boys in high school so we never had to compete over them. Love you, Phil. And I'm so thankful for you and how tremendously well you and the rest of that group loved Katy. Katy is our glue. I loved so much that my parents lived close to school so we were able to go watch 30 minutes of ABC Family while scarfing down bagel bites, goldfish dipped in Catalina dressing (why was that a thing, you're gross), Oreos over soaked and soggy in milk, and cookie dough from a giant bucket before soccer practice. Although, I used to get so pissed because you would always pick out the dough and leave me with a spoonful of chocolate chips. It's a miracle we didn't ever puke at practice. I think that may have had something to do with how insanely lazy we were. Remember when we used to jump in people's cars when we were supposed to be running a mile around the neighborhood? Did I ever tell you how I was always so jealous that you would score ALL our goals and have your name called over the intercom to the whole school the next day. I seriously could never keep up with you. Katy, I'm sorry Ruthie was always better at tennis than you. However, I am not sorry she was so much better than us at basketball. Can you imagine how many points Hoopin Squad would actually have scored in a game if Ruthie wasn't on our team?

So much of who I am, what I've done, and what my life has looked like since high school is directly correlated to having you as my best friend.

I am so grateful we have always stayed within driving distance of one another. I started playing ultimate because I was struggling in college, and you knew I needed an outlet for my competitive and active nature. You taught me how to throw a flick and catch a pancake, and you patiently and lovingly kept me accountable about following through with joining the team at UT... And then you bitches beat us EVERY SINGLE TIME we played one another for the next two years. You rubbed it in my face and then gave my whole team a drink. You loved so fully and so hard. You had such an amazing way of bringing people together. Have I mentioned that you're glue?

I moved to the northwest because of you, K. You had such a way of inspiring and sometimes forcing people to seek adventure. Every time you came to visit me in Portland the past 6 years I prepared for five things to happen.

1. Losing 1-2 articles of clothing. We all know you weren't

about to spend your time and money shopping. And even if you had, you have pretty awful fashion sense

2. You were going to eat all my food and drink my booze

3. You would clean my room

4. Non-stop adventures: She came on her 25th and made a list of 25 things to do for her 25th birthday that we had to fit into a two day weekend (including kick Lindsay's ass at ping pong)

5. Buying Destiny Ray jewelry. You wanted to support people you love

I feel so fortunate to have gotten to see glimpses into your life in Montana. You always showed me the best time in Missoula. You and your friends were so welcoming and truly made me feel a part of your friend group. They loved me well because they love you so much. Thank you for challenging me to be a better person and friend. Thank you for continuing to pursue me even when I wouldn't respond for weeks... Let's be honest, sometimes months. You were undoubtedly a better friend to me than I was to you. Thank you for teaching me tolerance. Thank you for demonstrating how to be a servant to others. Thank you for forcing me out of my comfort zone.

Katy, we had so much more to do. You already asked me to be in your hypothetical wedding. You were supposed to be in my wedding (again). You were going to be the crazy aunt to my kids. I was going to put up with your annoying dog and you would continue to secretly love my cats. We were going to hold one another as we lost people we love. We had so many more adventures to go on. We were going to grow old together and make fun of one another's sagging skin and deteriorating hearing.

KK, I'm sorry you were in so much pain. I know there is nothing any of us could do, but I hope you knew how loved you were. You brought so much happiness to all of us, and we are forever grateful for you. I hope we can all take a page out of your book and... I literally cannot figure out how to finish this sentence. I know everyone has something that they learned from Katy.

Katy, I want to promise you some things. Kate, Rachel, and I will keep going to Memphis Pizza Cafe when we are all in town and keep up with our email chain to continue to love one another from afar. I will keep in touch with Allie and love her and Jon as they settle into married life. I will visit your parents every time I come in town and hug them hard for you.

I promise to not get stuck in the why or what if game? You would want us all to only seek happiness and love.

I promise to think of you as I continue our bad habits of shells and cheese, ice cream, too much pizza, too many beers, etc.

I promise to keep listening to music that makes me happy and think of how much you would love it.

I promise to keep seeking adventures. I promise to make my bed...at least some of the time.

I promise to keep taking beers on my hikes.

I promise to keep riding my bike.

I promise to be a better friend.

Katy, you are our glue. We promise to hold firm together.

13: Grieving in Paradise

My son Jack, Katy's older brother, is a third-year medical student in Hawaii. He wrote this letter to me in February while working in obstetrics.

* * *

Glad you're getting lots of tennis and squash in. Play as much as you can. I've pretty much altogether dropped sports. It's really sad, but I hope to pick them back up at another time in my life.

I've been putting in a lot of hours during OB. Hours worked produces good evaluations which hopefully leads to a residency which one day may lead to a good career and a normal life. According to the attending doctors, life gets much easier after residency. We've had a lot of interesting work on labor and delivery and in the OR.

OB really brings out the rawest aspects of life. I had a patient who had a near-death post-operative hemorrhage. She bled almost her entire blood volume into her abdomen. It was a surgeon's error – but many factors play into surgery errors (not just the surgeon's skills). After she came around we talked and she was pretty emotional and decided to make plans to turn her life around. She even remembered my name the next morning and that I was holding her hand while the surgeon was trying to place a central line in her neck. I think about why I couldn't have held Katy's hand when she was on the brink, then brought her back like we did with this patient.

I had a patient with a nine-month fetus that we took into a crash c-section. This is when the fetus is starved of oxygen and must come out immediately. The surgeon opened the uterus and pulled out a pale, floppy baby that wasn't breathing or crying. The surgeon handed me the baby and told me to rub it with a blanket. "Take the baby to the warmer and don't drop it!" I whisked the baby to the pediatrics team in the room.

The next day I visited the mom. She was tired but she smiled and gave short answers to my questions. I thought she might have a disability and tried to apply that to her situation. I saw her again today. I asked about her mood and she said, "I'm good." I asked again if she was sad or if she had seen her baby. She cried, "My baby!" I realized she had been too tired, too confused, too filled with worry the day before to understand what was happening. Her baby was not well and would possibly die in the hospital or leave severely brain damaged. Her baby had been healthy and well for 39 weeks. In 20 minutes everything went wrong. I was reminded that tragedy is not uncommon but our grief is ours alone to share.

Catching babies is really neat and I get choked up seeing young couples starting new families. I tell them all how beautiful their baby is, I shake the mother and father's hand ritualistically, and get really caught up in how beautiful the moment is. I think of Katy all the time, especially in the mornings, and what it would be like to see her with a baby. I know she's at peace now and that we did everything for her.

This afternoon I met a 39-year-old woman with ovarian cancer. The cancer has spread throughout her body and there is nothing that we could do to cure her disease. When I met her she kind of desperately asked me, the medical student, to save her life. I told her we would take great care of her, but was careful not to say everything would be OK. The surgeon removed a baseball-sized tumor from her abdomen. It will allow her to be comfortable and in less pain and give her some time. I'll see her tomorrow morning and ask her more about her life.

I thought about how short life is. I think about how happy Katy was for most of her life. I am reminded to also remember these happy times.

14: Lessons from Gisela and Walter
(Pass Christian, January 25, 2017)

"Life is amazing, and then it's awful, and then it's amazing again."
—R. Knost, again.

"It is approaching the magic hour before sunset when all things are related."
—Walter Anderson in his Horn Island Log

* * *

At low tide on the Mississippi Sound at Pass Christian you can walk out a hundred yards or more on the spits and sandbars and never be in water deeper than your shins. The sand is pockmarked with crab holes, and you can see the wavy patterns that artist and naturalist Walter Anderson of Ocean Springs made famous in his work.

Ginny Stuckey has sort of been our adopted daughter since she came to Memphis in 2005 with Teach For America and lived with us for several weeks when we were empty-nesters. Now she travels with Penny, her golden-doodle that looks like a golden retriever with a perm of tight curls or a little boy in a dog costume.

Penny is a good water dog either way, and she bounded into the shallow Sound chasing her ball, seagulls, pelicans, or just for the hell of it. The water is cold in January but so shallow and clear that you want to take off your shoes and roll up your pants to wade in it anyway. There wasn't anyone else on the beach this morning, and the sun blasted off the white sand of the man-made beach. On a clear day the closest barrier island stands out so vividly that you can see individual trees. The French discovers named it Cat Island. They were misinformed. The kitties were racoons.

Looking at an island across a body of water is what made me decide to buy a second home in Pass Christian last year. I closed the deal on August 29th, the 11th anniversary of Hurricane Katrina, which seemed ominous, but at 67 what are you waiting for? The former owner of the house was an old lady named Gisela who grew up in Nazi Germany, survived Kristallnacht, and escaped to freedom during World War II. When I was scraping off the flowered wallpaper and ripping up the pink carpet all over the house, I invented a back story for her in which she vowed to herself that if she ever escaped the darkness of Nazi Germany she would some day live in a place filled with flowers and bright colors.

I planned for Katy to come here and decorate the guest bedroom and ride bikes and walk on the beach with me and play her ukulele in my old age. Now it hurts to be happy. But some day, this year or ten years from now, who knows, we will have a life again, and this place will be part of it.

Walter Anderson is to the Mississippi Coast as Henry Thoreau is to Walden Pond and Robert Frost is to New England – the creative archetype of a region, with the body of work to back it up. An eccentric who "loved to draw on walls" he painted the walls of the Ocean Springs Community Center in 1951 for the sum of $1. Today his original watercolors sell for $15,000. A Walter Anderson print is essential to a proper Mississippi beach house.

What has this to do with me and Katy? For one thing, Anderson was an adventurist. Today we would say he was into extreme sports, and with his rugged good looks he would be on the cover of *Outside* magazine. Thoreau marched to his own drummer, but Anderson went him one better. He rowed a skiff eights miles to Horn Island in the Sound, where he would camp for weeks while sketching the flora, fauna and reptiles. Once he tied himself to a tree so he could "realize" the force of a hurricane. Another time he conquered his fear to face down an alligator. And back on land, he liked to ride his one-speed bicycle hundreds of miles to North Carolina, Florida, New York, and Texas. Once he wound up in China and did not return to the coast for two years.

His friends and family thought Bob, as he was known, was a little nutty with this realization business, as indeed he was, with a stay or two in a mental hospital to prove it, but he was a great artist because he felt, saw, and knew things that normal people did not. He felt the pull of place as surely as most people feel the pull of gravity.

Six months ago I would have said that old Bob's musings about unseen connections with other souls and hearing the silence and all that was hooey. Now I think he was a sage, and I want to be more like him. I can't wait to take a boat to the barrier islands and camp out on the beach under the stars and see if, over time, I can nurture the kind of attachment to nature and place that Walter Anderson had to Horn Island and Katy had to Montana.

It is possible to have a life after horror and loss. Gisela lived 77 years after escaping the Nazis. Walter Anderson was most productive after escaping from the state mental hospital. Pass Christian completely rebuilt itself after deadly hurricanes in 1969 and 2005. I have hopes.

Acknowledgments

Contrary to popular belief, it isn't true that "there are no words." There is nothing more comforting to a suicide survivor than a thoughtful letter or note. I hope I never again hesitate to write one, or to sit tongue-tied with a grieving close friend. Thanks to all who wrote cards and letters whether or not they are excerpted in this book.

Moving on after suicide is a shaky proposition. Just as our resolve is tested every day, so are we randomly "saved" at trying times by what I can only describe as angels. Special thanks to the Stonewallers for being here, Rheta and Hines for sanctuary, first responders Charlie and Margaret, the tennis guys and ladies for getting us on the court, the squash guys, the floor angels Betty and David, lunch guys Henry and Mike and Charlie, and Scott and Sean and Suhair for refusing to let me pay.

The grief shelf at the library is a big one, and so is the one on suicide survivors. What comforts someone is, of course, a personal matter.

In the aftermath of Katy's death I was not able to concentrate enough to read at my normal rate and preferred to walk or do physical work, but these books were helpful: *God Laughs and Plays*, by David James Duncan, who lives near Missoula, Montana; *Blue Nights*, by Joan Didion, about the death of her daughter; *Waiting for the Morning Train*, Bruce Catton's Michigan boyhood memoir, especially the chapter about his father's death; *All the King's Men*, by Robert Penn Warren, for the last part about accepting the burden of the past; *Duane's Depressed*, a novel by Larry McMurtry, in which Duane moves out of his house and walks and bikes his way through grief and depression; *The Happiness Hypothesis*, by Jonathan Haidt, which summarizes a lot of ancient wisdom and 20th century psychology about depression, unhappiness, and happiness in about 250 pages; *Rules for Old Men Waiting*, by Peter Pouncey, a short novel about grief, depression, and old age; *Approaching the Magic Hour: Memories of Walter Anderson*, by Agnes Grinstead Anderson; and *My Son...My Son...*, by Iris Bolton, who is a suicidologist, something I wish I had never heard of.

Music was another matter. When I wasn't talking to myself, I could not get songs and melodies out of my head for hours. If there is a more mournful jazz ballad than "Pearls" by Sade or "Dear Lord" by John Coltrane I have not heard it. Katy and I had different tastes but I got hooked on "Decades" by The Lil' Smokies of Montana and "I'm Yours" by Jason Mraz because she liked them so much.

CPSIA information can be obtained
at www.ICGtesting.com
Printed in the USA
LVHW092355030720
659705LV00002B/10/J

9 780615 997889